easy masks to sew

contents

simple mask

Easy Masks to Sew
First Published in 2020 by Zakka Workshop,
a division of World Book Media, LLC

www.zakkaworkshop.com
134 Federal Street
Salem, MA 01970 USA

Ima sugu Tsukurou! Tedzukuri Mask ©2020 Boutique-sha
Zoho Kaiteiban Kantan Kawaii! Tedzukuri Mask (PBS no. 610)
©2013 Boutique-sha

Titles originally published in Japanese language
by Boutique-sha, Tokyo, Japan.

English language rights, translation & production
by World Book Media, LLC.

English edition design by Stacy Wakefield Forte

ISBN: 978-0-9853747-4-7

Printed in China
10 9 8 7 6 5 4 3 2 1

introduction

Wearing a mask can help prevent the spread of germs and protect against allergens, pollution, and harsh cleaning fumes. It's possible to purchase commercially made masks, but why not take the opportunity to make your own fabric masks that are both functional and attractive?

This collection includes designs for three basic mask styles that are easy to sew: simple, pleated, and contoured. Choose the mask design best suited for your personal preferences and comfort. Each mask style is available in different sizes so you can make masks for everyone in your family, from kids to adults. The kids size is designed for children up to 6 years*, while the medium size will be better suited for teens or adults with small faces. Sizes medium and large are designed for adults—select the size best suited for your individual needs.

When selecting fabric for masks, look for tightly woven fabrics, such as quilting cotton. Remember to prewash your fabric before you start sewing. As an added bonus, the book also includes enough elastic to make three masks, so you can get started sewing right away!

DISCLAIMER While fabric masks are not guaranteed to protect against the transmission of viruses, the CDC recommends wearing them to slow the spread of viruses and help people who may have a virus and do not know it from transmitting it to others. Cloth face masks are not a replacement for medical grade personal protective equipment, and in circumstances where medical grade personal protective equipment is recommended, you should consult a health care professional. Follow the latest advice of the CDC and your own health care professionals as to how best to keep yourself safe. Visit the CDC for more information: www.cdc.gov

* Cloth face coverings should not be placed on young children under age 2, anyone who has trouble breathing, or is unconscious, incapacitated or otherwise unable to remove the mask without assistance.

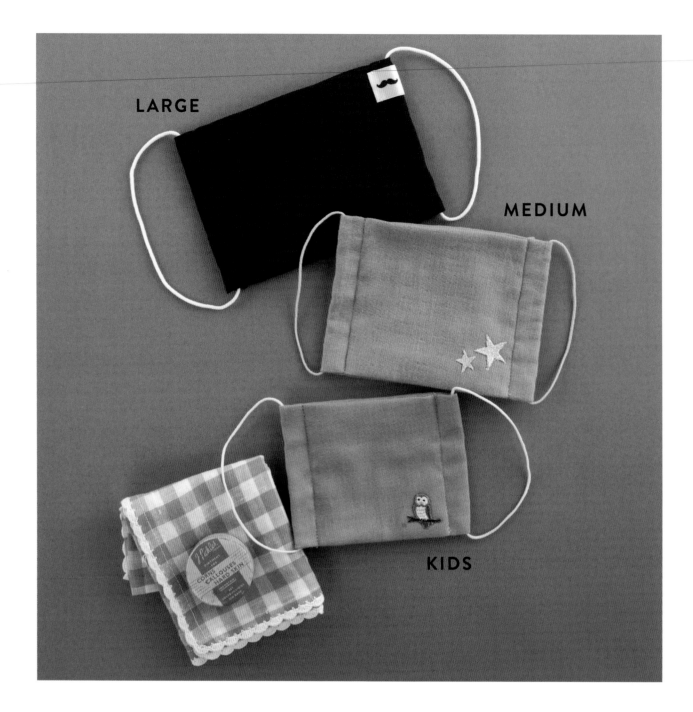

LARGE

MEDIUM

KIDS

simple mask

This basic mask can be made just by sewing straight lines.
It features three layers of fabric. When selecting fabrics,
try quilting cotton or use old clothing or household linens.

materials

	KIDS	MEDIUM	LARGE
FABRIC	13 x 7½ in (33 x 19 cm)	17¼ x 8¾ in (44 x 22 cm)	18¾ x 9¾ in (47.5 x 25 cm)
ELASTIC	20 in (50 cm)	24 in (60 cm)	24 in (60 cm)
FINISHED SIZE	4½ x 3½ in (11 x 9 cm)	6 x 4 in (15 x 10 cm)	6½ x 4¾ in (16.5 x 12 cm)

cutting directions

- Cut the mask using the dimensions listed below.

NOTE: THESE DIMENSIONS INCLUDE SEAM ALLOWANCE.

KIDS

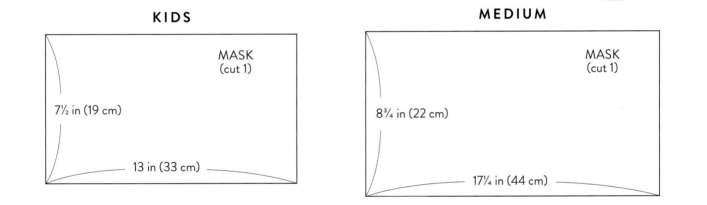

MASK
(cut 1)

7½ in (19 cm)

13 in (33 cm)

MEDIUM

MASK
(cut 1)

8¾ in (22 cm)

17¼ in (44 cm)

LARGE

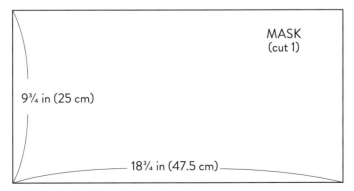

MASK
(cut 1)

9¾ in (25 cm)

18¾ in (47.5 cm)

instructions

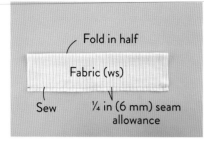

1 Fold the fabric in half with right sides together. Sew together along the bottom edge using ¼ in (6 mm) seam allowance.

2 Turn right side out. Press so that the seam line is just visible on the inside of the mask, but not seen on the outside.

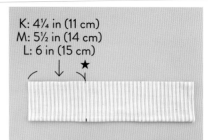

3 Measure from the left edge and mark the fold line at the location noted by the ★. Use the measurement listed in the photo above.

4 Next, measure from the ★ and mark another fold line at the location noted by the ☆. Use the measurement listed in the photo above.

5 Fold along the line marked with the ★. Press using the iron.

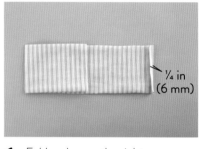

6 Fold and press the right raw edge ¼ in (6 mm).

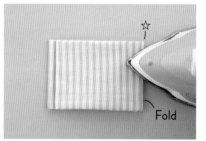

7 Fold along the line marked with the ☆. Press using the iron.

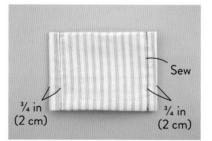

8 Topstitch the left and right edges using ¾ in (2 cm) seam allowance. This will create channels for the elastic.

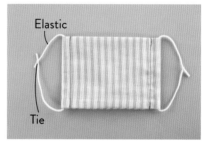

9 Cut the elastic in half. Insert pieces of elastic through the channels made in step 8 and tie into loops. Check the fit and adjust the size of the elastic loops if necessary. Adjust the elastic to hide the knots inside the channels and complete the mask.

LARGE

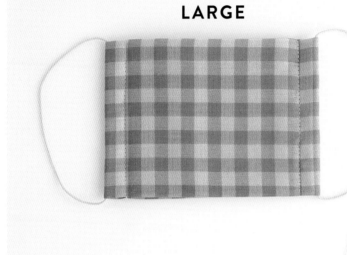

MEDIUM

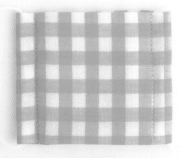

KIDS

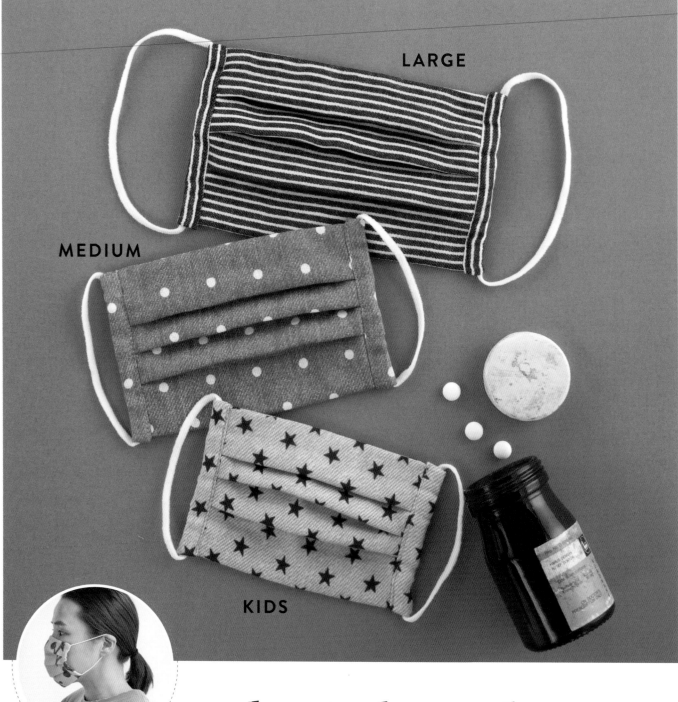

LARGE

MEDIUM

KIDS

pleated mask

This versatile mask allows you to expand the pleats to adjust the coverage.
There's even an option to insert a wire for a more customized fit along the nose.

materials

	KIDS	MEDIUM	LARGE
FABRIC	16 x 8 in (40 x 20 cm)	18 x 8 in (45 x 20 cm)	20 x 10 in (50 x 25 cm)
ELASTIC	20 in (50 cm)	24 in (60 cm)	24 in (60 cm)
FINISHED SIZE	5¼ x 3¼ in (13.5 x 8 cm)	6¼ x 3¾ in (15.5 x 9 cm)	7 x 4 in (17.5 x 10 cm)

cutting directions

- Use the templates on pages 12–14 to cut out the outside and lining.
- Use the dimensions listed below to cut out the bindings.

	KIDS	MEDIUM	LARGE
BINDING	3¾ x 1¾ in (9.7 x 4.2 cm)	4¼ x 1¾ in (10.7 x 4.2 cm)	4½ x 1¾ in (11.2 x 4.2 cm)

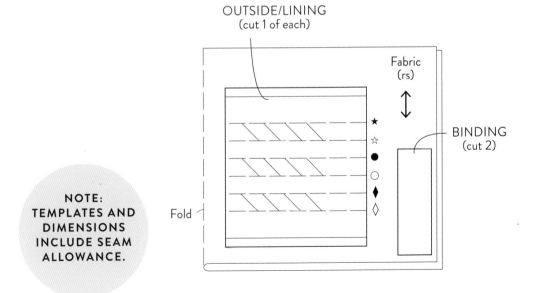

OUTSIDE/LINING
(cut 1 of each)

Fabric
(rs)

BINDING
(cut 2)

Fold

NOTE:
TEMPLATES AND
DIMENSIONS
INCLUDE SEAM
ALLOWANCE.

instructions

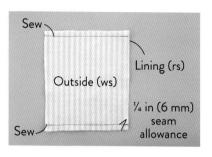

1 Align the outside and lining with right sides together. Sew together along the top and bottom using ¼ in (6 mm) seam allowance.

2 Turn right side out and press into shape using the iron.

OPTIONAL NOSE WIRE

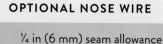
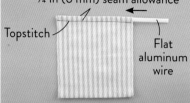

For a more customized fit, try using a piece of flat aluminum wire or a pipe cleaner along the nose area. If using the nose wire, topstitch ¼ in (6 mm) from the top to create a channel. Insert a 3½ in (9 cm) piece of wire into the channel.

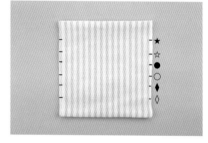

3 Mark the pleat lines as noted on the template.

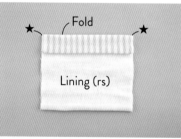

4 Fold along the ★ and press the crease.

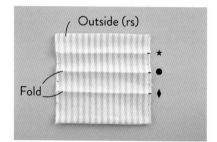

5 Follow the same process to fold and press creases along the ● and ♦ marks.

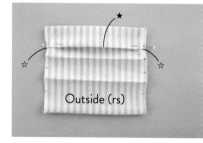

6 To fold the first pleat, align the ★ crease line on top of the ☆ marks. Pin in place.

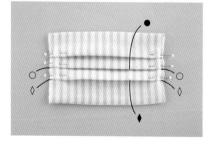

7 Follow the same process to fold the second and third pleats by aligning the ● crease line on top of the ○ marks and the ♦ crease line on top of the ◊ marks.

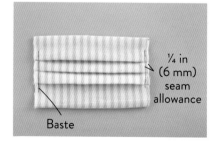

8 Use a long stitch length to baste the pleats in place along the left and right edges of the mask using ¼ in (6 mm) seam allowance.

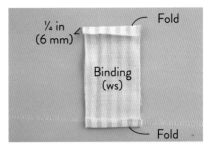

9 Fold and press the top and bottom edges of each binding piece over ¼ in (6 mm) to the wrong side.

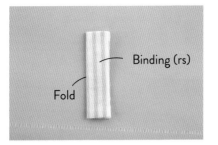

10 Next, fold each binding piece in half widthwise and press. This will create a crease line to mark where the binding will wrap around the edge of the mask.

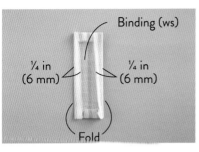

11 Open each binding piece along the fold made in step 10. Fold and press the left and right edges over ¼ in (6 mm) to the wrong side.

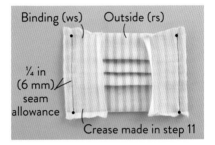

12 Open each binding piece completely flat. With right sides together, sew the binding pieces to the left and right edges of the mask. Use ¼ in (6 mm) seam allowance so you'll be sewing along the crease lines made in step 11. Make sure to start and stop sewing ¼ in (6 mm) in from the top and bottom edge of the binding piece.

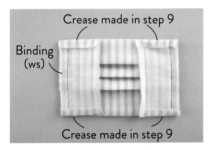

13 Fold and press the top and bottom edges of the binding pieces over ¼ in (6 mm) to the wrong side along the crease lines made in step 9.

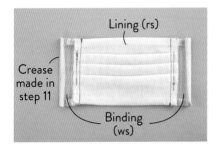

14 Flip the mask over so the lining is facing up. Fold and press the remaining raw edges of the binding pieces over ¼ in (6 mm) to the wrong side along the crease lines made in step 11.

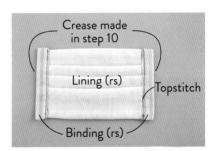

15 Fold the binding pieces along the crease lines made in step 10, covering the seam allowance. Topstitch the bindings in place, stitching as close to the edge as possible.

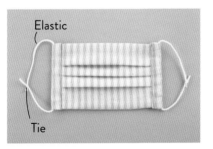

16 Cut the elastic in half. Insert pieces of elastic through the bindings and tie into loops. Check the fit and adjust the size of the elastic loops if necessary.

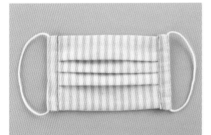

17 Adjust the elastic to hide the knots inside the bindings and complete the mask.

full-size templates

NOTE There are no templates for the bindings. Refer to the dimensions provided on page 9.

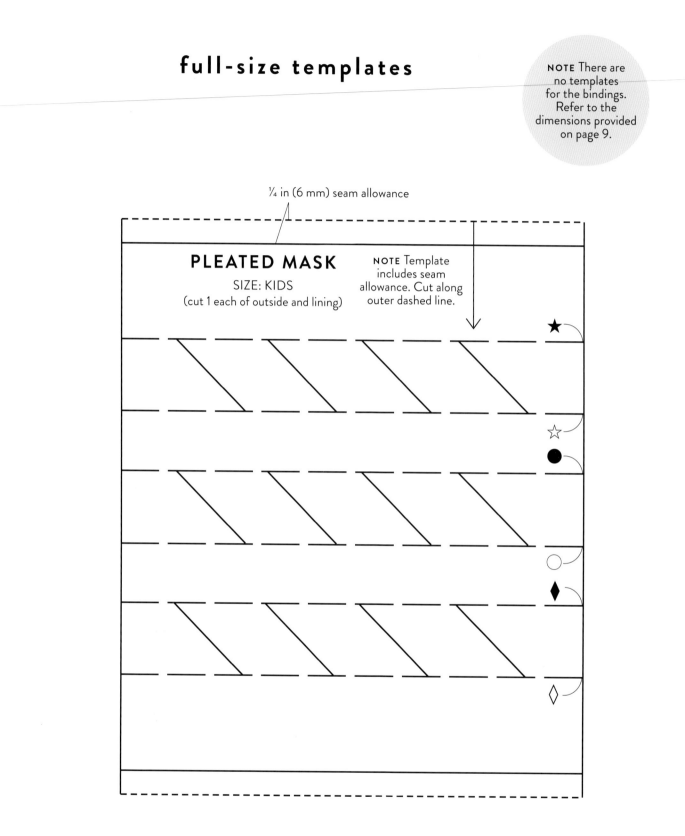

¼ in (6 mm) seam allowance

PLEATED MASK

SIZE: KIDS
(cut 1 each of outside and lining)

NOTE Template includes seam allowance. Cut along outer dashed line.

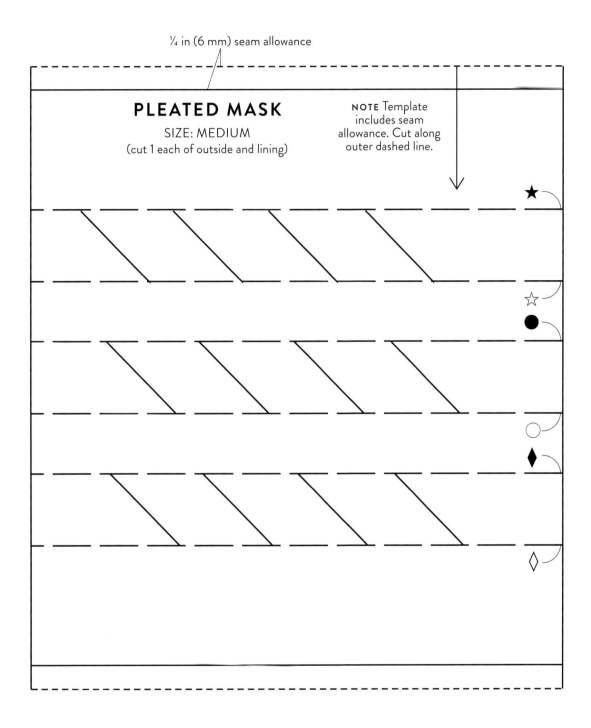

PLEATED MASK

SIZE: MEDIUM
(cut 1 each of outside and lining)

¼ in (6 mm) seam allowance

NOTE Template
includes seam
allowance. Cut along
outer dashed line.

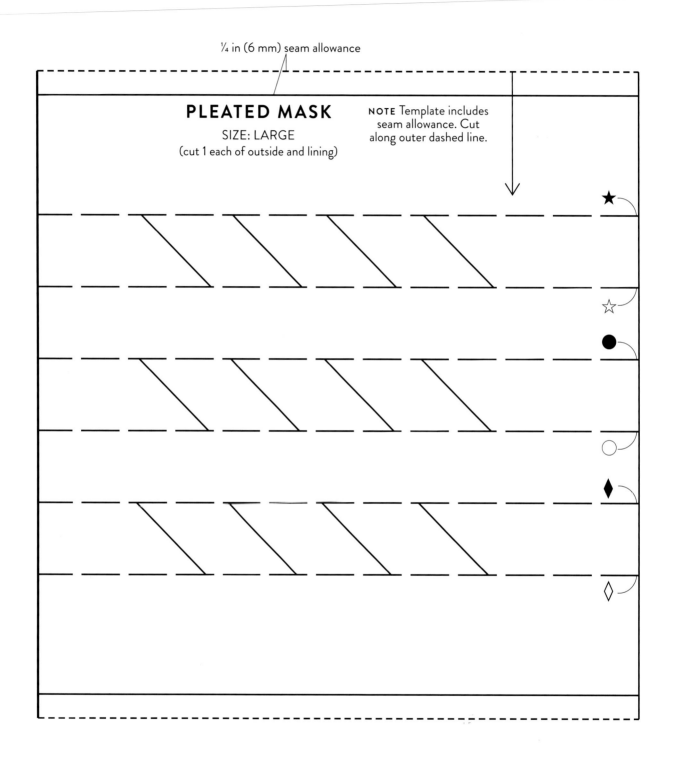

¼ in (6 mm) seam allowance

PLEATED MASK
SIZE: LARGE
(cut 1 each of outside and lining)

NOTE Template includes seam allowance. Cut along outer dashed line.

For added style, try using a contrasting fabric for the binding, such as the denim shown here. When using a print fabric, such as the striped double gauze shown here, note how the direction changes based on the fabric orientation.

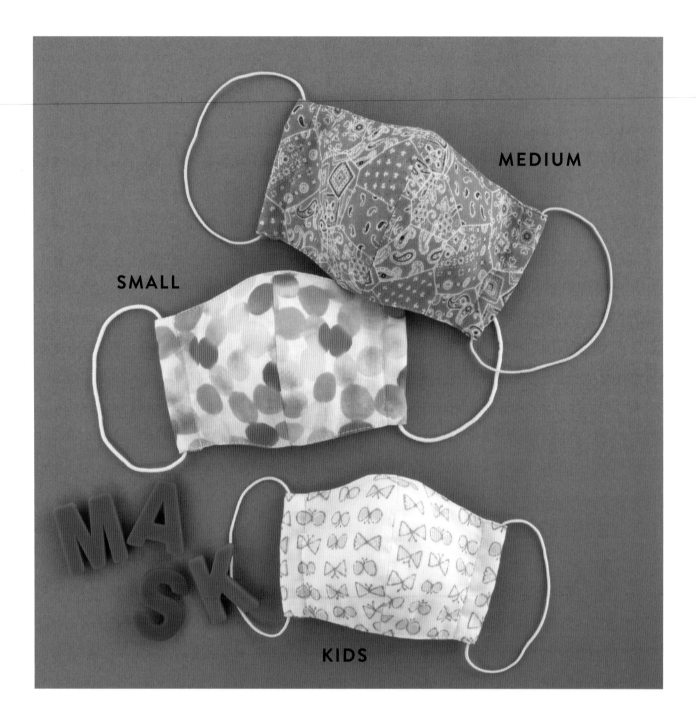

MEDIUM

SMALL

KIDS

contour mask

This three-dimensional mask style molds to the shape of your face and is comfortable to wear. Don't be intimidated by the convex shape—it's easier to sew than it looks!

materials

	KIDS	SMALL*	MEDIUM	LARGE
FABRIC	12 x 8 in (30 x 20 cm)	14 x 8 in (36 x 20 cm)	16 x 10 in (41 x 25 cm)	18 x 10 in (46 x 25 cm)
ELASTIC	20 in (50 cm)	24 in (60 cm)	24 in (60 cm)	24 in (60 cm)
FINISHED SIZE	6 x 4¼ in (15 x 11 cm)	6¾ x 4¾ in (17 x 12 cm)	8 x 5¼ in (20 x 13 cm)	8½ x 7 in (21.5 x 18 cm)

* The small is intended for older children ages 6-12.

cutting directions

- Use the templates on pages 20–22 to cut out two outsides and two linings.

NOTE:
TEMPLATES
INCLUDE
SEAM
ALLOWANCE.

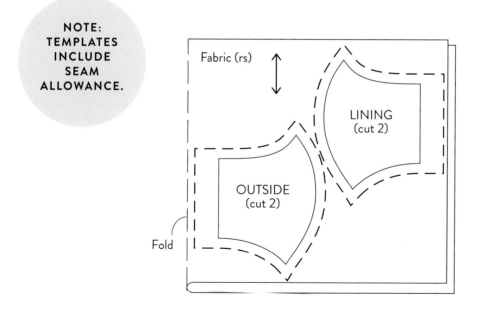

instructions

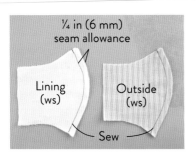

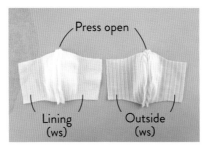

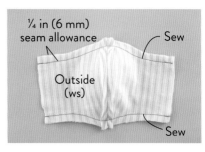

1 Align the two outside pieces with right sides together. Sew together along the curve using ¼ in (6 mm) seam allowance. Repeat with the two lining pieces.

2 Press the seam allowances open.

3 Align the outside and lining with right sides together. Sew together along the top and bottom edges using ¼ in (6 mm) seam allowance.

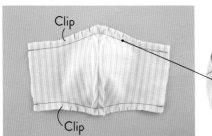

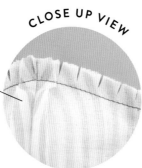

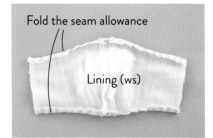

4 Make clips into the seam allowance along the curved section of the top and bottom. Make sure not to cut through the stitching.

5 Fold and press the top and bottom seam allowance toward the lining.

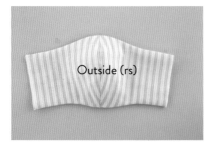

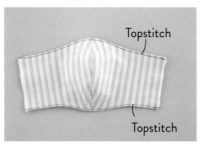

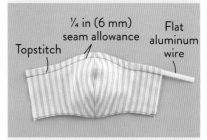

6 Turn right side out.

7 Topstitch the outside along the top and bottom, stitching as close to the edge as possible.

OPTIONAL NOSE WIRE

For a more customized fit, try using a piece of flat aluminum wire or a pipe cleaner along the nose area. If using the nose wire, topstitch ¼ in (6 mm) from the top to create a channel. Insert a 3½ in (9 cm) piece of wire into the channel.

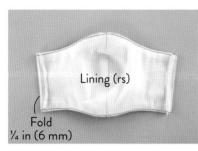

Lining (rs)

Fold
¼ in (6 mm)

8 Fold and press the left and right edges over ¼ in (6 mm) toward the lining.

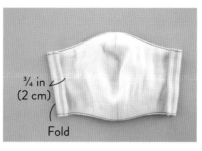

¾ in (2 cm)

Fold

9 Next, fold and press these edges over ¾ in (2 cm) toward the lining.

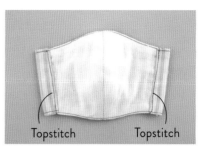

Topstitch   Topstitch

10 Topstitch the left and right edges, stitching as close to the edge as possible. This will create channels for the elastic.

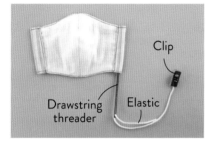

Clip

Drawstring threader   Elastic

11 Cut the elastic in half. Insert pieces of elastic through the channels made in step 10.

TIP Use a drawstring threader or tapestry needle to insert the elastic through the channel. You can attach a binding clip to the end of the elastic to keep the entire piece from being pulled through the channel.

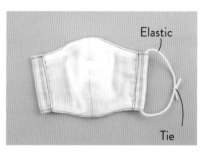

Elastic

Tie

12 Tie the elastic into loops. Check the fit and adjust the size of the loops if necessary.

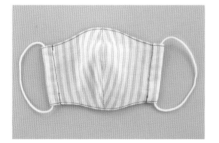

13 Adjust the elastic to hide the knots inside the channels and complete the mask.

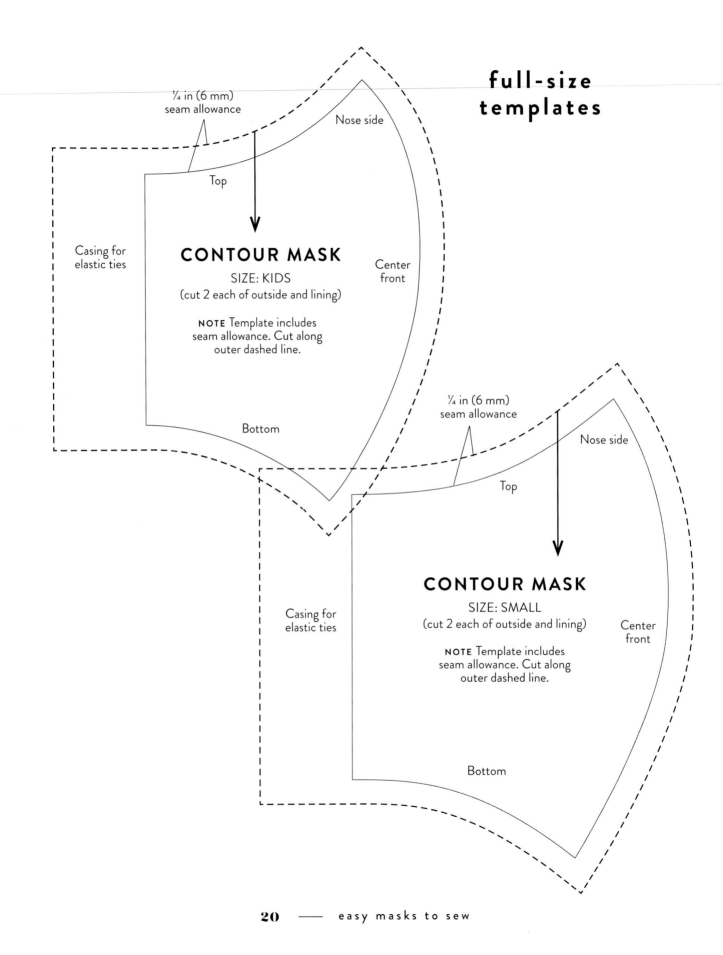

full-size
templates

¼ in (6 mm)
seam allowance

Nose side

Top

Casing for
elastic ties

CONTOUR MASK

SIZE: KIDS
(cut 2 each of outside and lining)

Center
front

NOTE Template includes
seam allowance. Cut along
outer dashed line.

Bottom

¼ in (6 mm)
seam allowance

Nose side

Top

Casing for
elastic ties

CONTOUR MASK

SIZE: SMALL
(cut 2 each of outside and lining)

Center
front

NOTE Template includes
seam allowance. Cut along
outer dashed line.

Bottom

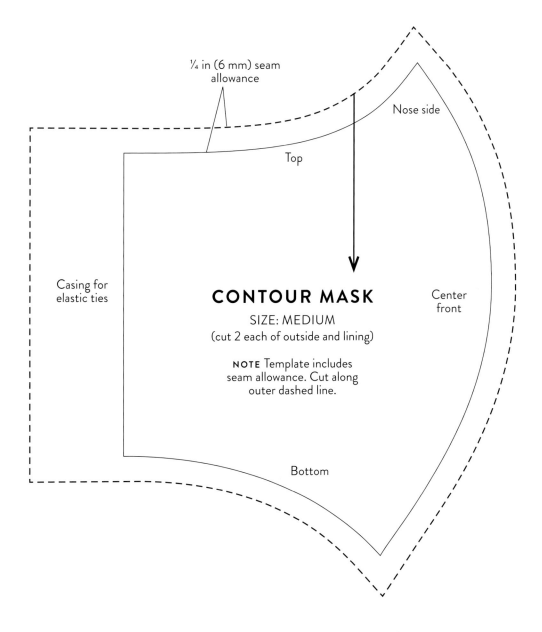

¼ in (6 mm) seam allowance

Nose side

Top

Casing for elastic ties

CONTOUR MASK

SIZE: MEDIUM
(cut 2 each of outside and lining)

NOTE Template includes seam allowance. Cut along outer dashed line.

Center front

Bottom

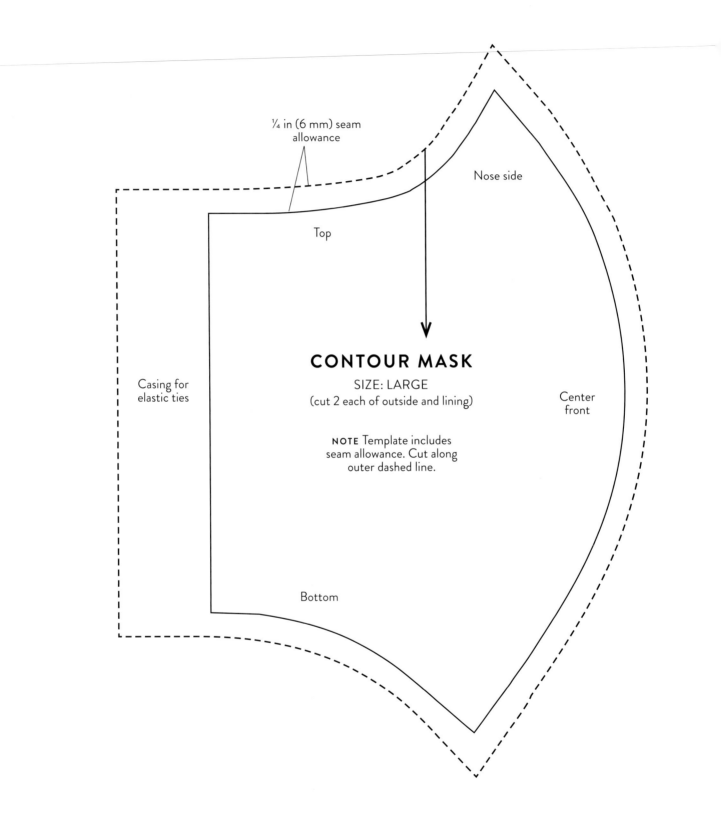

¼ in (6 mm) seam allowance

Nose side

Top

Casing for elastic ties

CONTOUR MASK

SIZE: LARGE
(cut 2 each of outside and lining)

NOTE Template includes seam allowance. Cut along outer dashed line.

Center front

Bottom

The three-dimensional shape of this mask design allows for more breathability, making this style mask an excellent choice for when you plan to wear it for an extended period of time.

KIDS

SMALL

MEDIUM

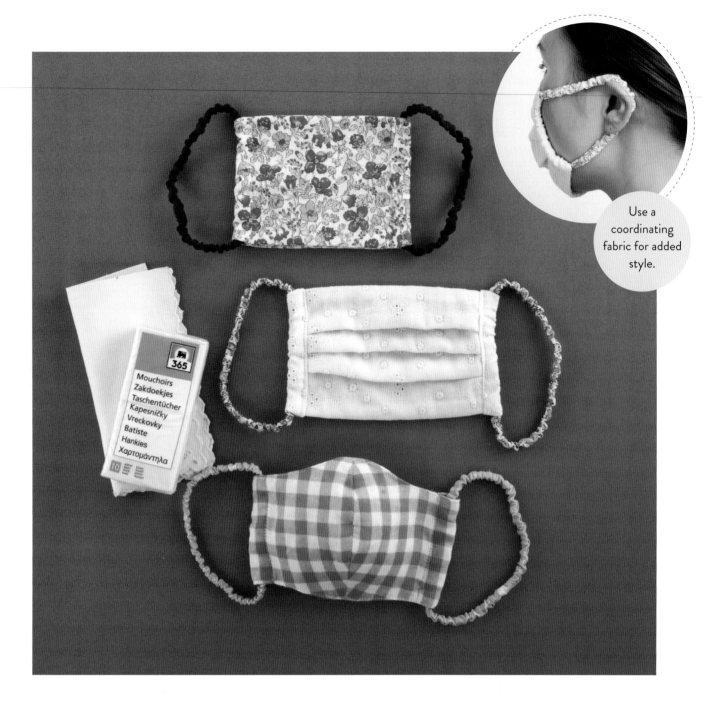

fabric covered ties

Use this tutorial to make fabric tubes for the elastic ties. The fabric will keep the elastic from digging into your skin and is helpful for those wearing a mask for an extended period of time.

materials

FABRIC	13 ¾ x 4 in (35 x 10 cm)
ELASTIC	24 in (60 cm)
FINISHED SIZE	Two 12 in (30 cm) ties

NOTE You may need to adjust amount of elastic/length of fabric for smaller ties (for kids).

cutting directions

- Cut 2 fabric tubes using the dimensions listed below.

NOTE These dimensions include seam allowance.

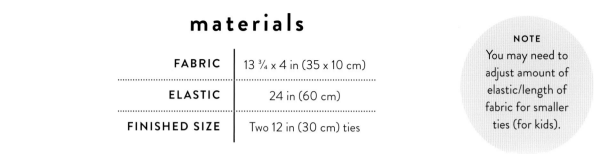

1 in (2.5 cm)

FABRIC TUBE (cut 2)

12 in (30 cm)

instructions

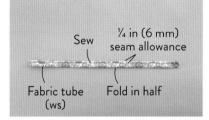

Sew · ¼ in (6 mm) seam allowance · Fabric tube (ws) · Fold in half

1 Fold the fabric in half with right sides together. Sew from end to end to create a tube, using ¼ in (6 mm) seam allowance.

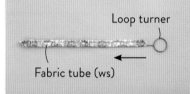

Loop turner · Fabric tube (ws)

2 Insert a loop turner into the tube. Hook the latched end of the loop turner onto the end of the fabric tube.

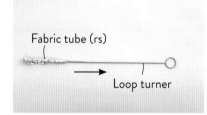

Fabric tube (rs) · Loop turner

3 Pull the loop turner back through the fabric tube, turning it right side out.

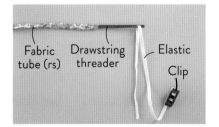

Fabric tube (rs) · Drawstring threader · Elastic · Clip

4 Cut the elastic into two pieces. Use a drawstring threader or safety pin to insert the elastic through the fabric tube. It helps to attach a binding clip or safety pin to the end of the elastic to prevent the entire piece from being pulled through the fabric tube.

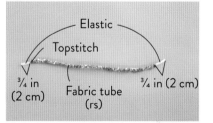

Elastic · Topstitch · ¾ in (2 cm) · Fabric tube (rs) · ¾ in (2 cm)

5 Pull the elastic so it extends ¾ in (2 cm) from each end of the fabric tube. Topstitch in place as shown above.

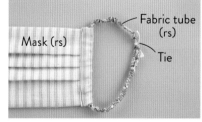

Mask (rs) · Fabric tube (rs) · Tie

6 Insert the fabric covered elastic through the channels of the mask. Tie the ends of the elastic into loops. Adjust the elastic to hide the knots inside the channels.

puppy, cat & bear masks

These friendly faces are sure to make wearing a mask more fun
for your little ones! Make a simple mask as shown on page 5, then
appliqué and embroider faces to create a puppy, cat, or bear.

materials

PUPPY

	KIDS
MASK FABRIC	13 x 7½ in (33 x 19 cm)
BROWN FABRIC	6 x 4 in (15 x 10 cm)
LIGHT BROWN FABRIC	4 x 2 in (10 x 5 cm)
ELASTIC	20 in (50 cm)
EMBROIDERY THREAD	No. 25 in dark brown
STUFFING	Small tuft
FINISHED SIZE	4½ x 3½ in (11 x 9 cm)

HOW TO APPLIQUÉ

1
Trace the finished size template onto thick paper and cut out

2 ¼ in (6 mm) seam allowance
Thick paper
Appliqué fabric (ws)

3 Clip
Thick paper
Fold and press seam allowance

4
Stitch to background fabric, removing thick paper as you work

instructions

1 Make a kids size simple mask following instructions on pages 5–6.

2 Appliqué and embroider the face as noted below. Use the templates on the right. Refer to page 29 for instructions on making the nose.

full-size templates

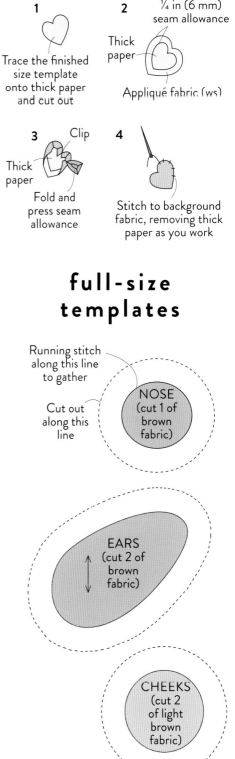

Running stitch along this line to gather

Cut out along this line

NOSE (cut 1 of brown fabric)

EARS (cut 2 of brown fabric)

CHEEKS (cut 2 of light brown fabric)

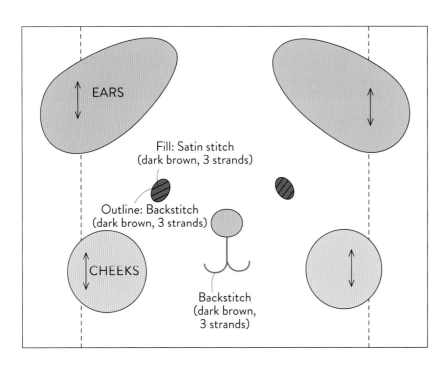

EARS

Fill: Satin stitch (dark brown, 3 strands)

Outline: Backstitch (dark brown, 3 strands)

CHEEKS

Backstitch (dark brown, 3 strands)

materials

CAT

	KIDS
MASK FABRIC	13 x 7½ in (33 x 19 cm)
LIGHT PINK FABRIC	4 x 2 in (10 x 5 cm)
LIGHT BROWN FABRIC	4 x 2 in (10 x 5 cm)
BROWN FABRIC	2 x 2 in (5 x 5 cm)
ELASTIC	20 in (50 cm)
EMBROIDERY THREAD	No. 25 in dark brown and purple
STUFFING	Small tuft
FINISHED SIZE	4½ x 3½ in (11 x 9 cm)

instructions

1 Make a kids size simple mask following instructions on pages 5–6.

2 Appliqué and embroider the face as noted below. Use the templates on the right. Refer to page 27 for appliqué instructions and page 29 for instructions on making the nose.

full-size templates

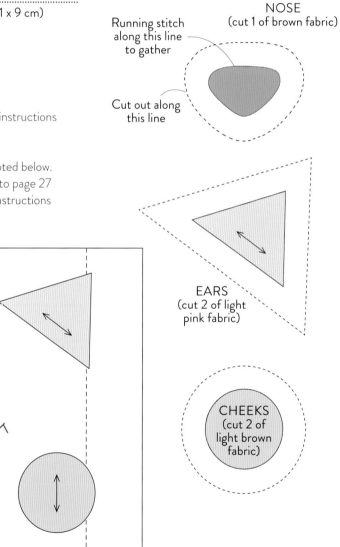

Running stitch along this line to gather

NOSE
(cut 1 of brown fabric)

Cut out along this line

EARS
(cut 2 of light pink fabric)

CHEEKS
(cut 2 of light brown fabric)

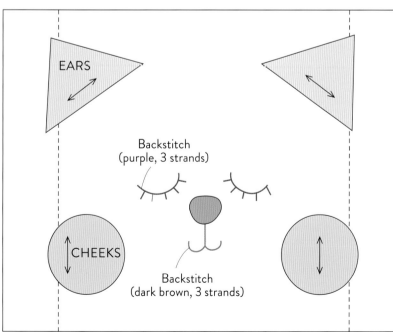

EARS

Backstitch
(purple, 3 strands)

CHEEKS

Backstitch
(dark brown, 3 strands)

materials

BEAR

	KIDS
MASK FABRIC	13 x 7½ in (33 x 19 cm)
DARK BROWN FABRIC	4 x 4 in (10 x 10 cm)
LIGHT BROWN FABRIC	4 x 2 in (10 x 5 cm)
ELASTIC	20 in (50 cm)
EMBROIDERY THREAD	No. 25 in dark brown
STUFFING	Small tuft
FINISHED SIZE	4½ x 3½ in (11 x 9 cm)

HOW TO MAKE THE NOSE

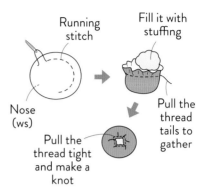

Running stitch

Fill it with stuffing

Nose (ws)

Pull the thread tight and make a knot

Pull the thread tails to gather

instructions

1 Make a kids size simple mask following instructions on pages 5–6.

2 Appliqué and embroider the face as noted below. Use the templates on the right. Refer to page 27 for appliqué instructions.

full-size templates

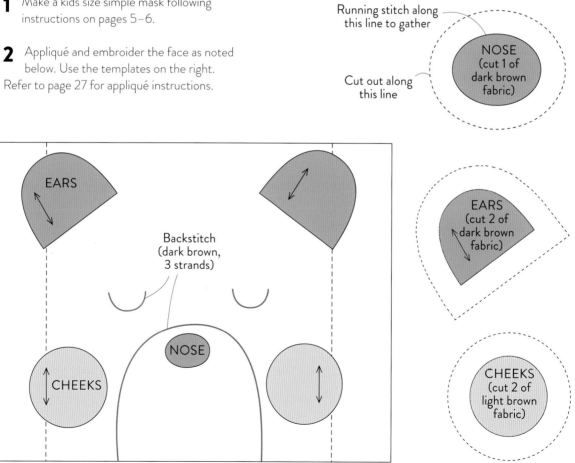

Running stitch along this line to gather

Cut out along this line

NOSE (cut 1 of dark brown fabric)

EARS (cut 2 of dark brown fabric)

CHEEKS (cut 2 of light brown fabric)

EARS

Backstitch (dark brown, 3 strands)

NOSE

CHEEKS

panda & duck masks

These adorable animal masks will make you smile!
Choose from a friendly panda or duck.

materials

PANDA

	KIDS
WHITE FABRIC	10 x 4 in (25 x 10 cm)
BLACK FABRIC	8 x 4 in (20 x 10 cm)
ELASTIC	16 in (40 cm)
EMBROIDERY THREAD	No. 25 in black and white
FINISHED SIZE	3¼ x 4¼ in (8.5 x 10.8 cm) including ears

DUCK

	KIDS
YELLOW FABRIC	10 x 4 in (25 x 10 cm)
ORANGE FABRIC	4 x 2 in (10 x 5 cm)
ELASTIC	16 in (40 cm)
EMBROIDERY THREAD	No. 25 in dark brown
FINISHED SIZE	3¼ x 4¼ in (8.2 x 10.8 cm)

instructions

PANDA

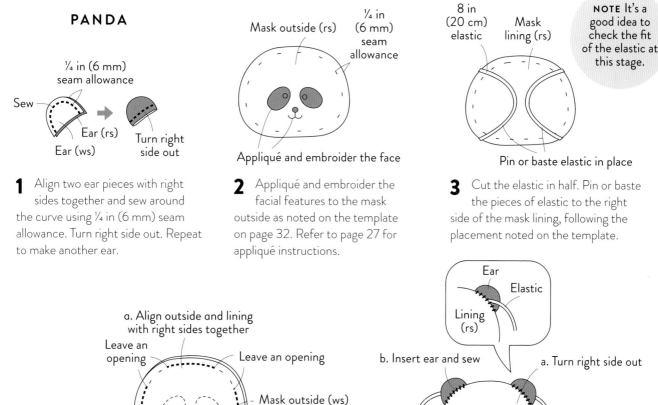

¼ in (6 mm) seam allowance

Sew

Ear (ws)   Ear (rs)

Turn right side out

Mask outside (rs)

¼ in (6 mm) seam allowance

Appliqué and embroider the face

8 in (20 cm) elastic   Mask lining (rs)

Pin or baste elastic in place

NOTE It's a good idea to check the fit of the elastic at this stage.

a. Align outside and lining with right sides together

Leave an opening   Leave an opening

Mask outside (ws)

b. Sew, leaving openings

Ear   Elastic   Lining (rs)

b. Insert ear and sew   a. Turn right side out

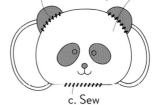

c. Sew

1 Align two ear pieces with right sides together and sew around the curve using ¼ in (6 mm) seam allowance. Turn right side out. Repeat to make another ear.

2 Appliqué and embroider the facial features to the mask outside as noted on the template on page 32. Refer to page 27 for appliqué instructions.

3 Cut the elastic in half. Pin or baste the pieces of elastic to the right side of the mask lining, following the placement noted on the template.

4 Align the mask outside and lining with right sides together. Sew together around the outline using ¼ in (6 mm) seam allowance, leaving openings at the ears and bottom.

5 Turn right side out. Insert the ears into the openings at the top of the mask and hand stitch closed. Fold the seam allowance in along the bottom opening and hand stitch closed.

full-size templates

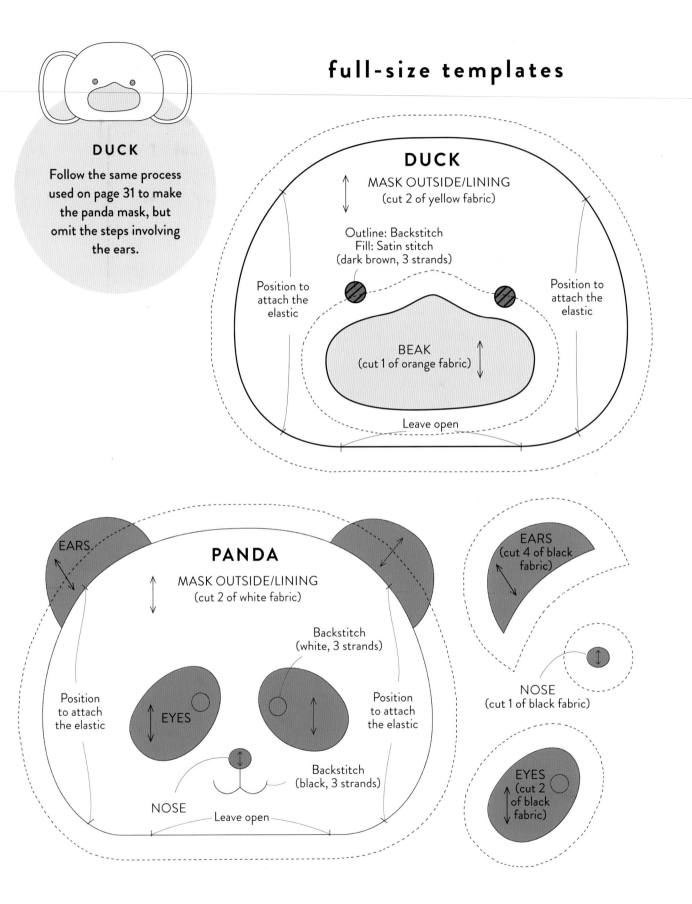

DUCK

Follow the same process used on page 31 to make the panda mask, but omit the steps involving the ears.

DUCK

MASK OUTSIDE/LINING
(cut 2 of yellow fabric)

Outline: Backstitch
Fill: Satin stitch
(dark brown, 3 strands)

Position to attach the elastic

Position to attach the elastic

BEAK
(cut 1 of orange fabric)

Leave open

PANDA

MASK OUTSIDE/LINING
(cut 2 of white fabric)

EARS

Backstitch
(white, 3 strands)

Position to attach the elastic

Position to attach the elastic

EYES

Backstitch
(black, 3 strands)

NOSE

Leave open

EARS
(cut 4 of black fabric)

NOSE
(cut 1 of black fabric)

EYES
(cut 2 of black fabric)